SEVEN
BIBLICAL
PRINCIPLES
TO LIVE BY

SAKEANAH JOHNSON

ISBN 978-1-68526-107-8 (Paperback)
ISBN 978-1-68526-108-5 (Digital)

Covenant Books, Inc.
11661 Hwy 707
Murrells Inlet, SC 29576
www.covenantbooks.com

INTRODUCTION

◈

Why Did I Get Saved?

As I sit here pondering the answer to the above question, first, I feel the need to explain what is being saved, why do I need salvation and what are the steps to receiving salvation. In the book of Genesis 2:16–17, we see that God has given Adam (the first man) a commandment. It reads, "And the Lord God commanded the man, saying, Of every tree of the garden thou mayest freely eat: But of the tree of the knowledge of good and evil, thou shalt not eat of it: for in the day that thou eatest thereof thou shall surely die."

God was specific and clear on His instructions to Adam. Adam was in a place where he had to work for nothing. His job was to have dominion (rule) over the fish of the sea, and over the cattle, and over all the earth, and over every creeping thing that creepeth upon the earth (Genesis 1:26). Adam and his wife Eve were also given authority by God and commanded to be fruitful, and multiply and replenish the earth,

3

and subdue it: and have dominion over the fish of the sea, and over the fowl of the air, and over every living thing that moveth upon the earth (Genesis 1:28). Adam and Eve had it made! They didn't have to work or toil. They didn't know hard labor, pain, or despair. They had all that they'd ever need or want already prepared for them before they were formed! God had prepared everything that they would need and then He brought them into the garden. Adam and Eve had every kind of plant that you can imagine, they had all kinds of herbs from the fields, and fruit for food. They were truly living it up! Adam had a wife, companion, a mate that God created just for him. But most importantly, he had communion daily with Almighty God. What else could Adam and Eve possibly want? They surely didn't lack anything because God saw to it. In chapter 3 of Genesis, we're introduced to another character. He is identified as the serpent. The serpent (deceiver) introduces doubt to the woman, and in return, Adam and Eve disobey God. They have broken the one commandment God gave them. As a result of their actions, sin enters the world. Their sin now brings a separation between God and man. The closeness is no longer there. Man is now driven out of the garden and we are introduced to the concept of hiding, guilt, shame, fear, discord, spiritual warfare between the woman and the serpent, the man having rulership (headship) over the woman, sorrow during childbirth, the ground is now cursed. Man will now return back to the dust, thorns and thistles are now a part of life and hard work for food. All of these things are a result of disobeying God. Man sinned against God. Sin means simply miss the mark. Man missed the mark that God set forth. Salvation is simply deliverance from sin and its consequences. Because the first man sinned, subsequently, we're all born sinners. The Bible tells us in Romans 5:12, "Wherefore, as by one man sin entered the world, and death by sin; and so death passed upon all men, for that all have sinned." In God's love for man and Him wanting to repair the breach with man, God offered us a way to restore fellowship and relationship. We are told in Romans 6:23, "For the wages (cost) of sin is death; but the gift of God is eternal life through Jesus Christ our Lord." Now that death is the payment for sin, someone would have to die. But who? Who was worthy? Who is without sin, spot, wrinkle, or blemish? Who is pure, holy, and righteous? Who can take the sting out of death, sin and the grave? Who could take back the keys of death (Revelation 1:18). His name is Jesus Christ! In John 3:16, the Bible tells us, "For God so loved the world, that he gave his only begotten Son, that whosoever believeth in him should not perish, but have everlasting life!" The breach is repaired through believing in Jesus. If thou shall confess with thou mouth the Lord Jesus, and shalt believe in thine heart that God has raised him from the dead, thou shall be saved. This is what it means to be saved. Being saved means that I've accepted God's gift, which is His only begotten Son, my sins are forgiven and now I have everlasting life. For with the heart man believeth unto righteousness: and with the mouth confession is made unto salvation (Romans 10:10). Now that we have an understanding of what salvation is, we arrive at the title of this section. Why did I get saved?

I have never really thought about this question as I did on the evening of July 22, 2017, as I sat in a church service. There was a prominent pastor who traveled between Dallas and Oklahoma at the time having a crusade. She posed a question to the audience, "Why did you get saved?" The audience responded with as many answers as there were people. To my surprise, the most common response to the question was "Because I didn't want to go to hell." As I began to ponder the thought for my own life, I took a trip back down memory lane. I thought back to the day when Christ really made since to me. My aha moment some twenty years ago. I was around twenty years old. It was a sunny day. I was attending a Sabbath keeping church at the time. I was also a college student. I have been "in church" nearly my whole life, going back as far as I can remember. Attending a Baptist church (my first recollection) around the age of three or four with our then next-door neighbor, Ms. Mattie Johnson. Later, we began attending Evangelist Temple Church of God in Christ when I was probably six years old or so. During that time, I enjoyed church so much. It was like my favorite place to be. At an early age, I had a zeal for the Lord. I was drawn to him. I attended YPWW (Young People Willing Workers) class under the teaching of Sister Mary Robinson and I truly loved learning about

God. It brought me a joy that was like nothing else. I would raise my hands anxiously and with exuberance to answer all of the questions. I didn't know that this was the beginning of having a relationship with God. As I sat on the second church pew with my mom, as a young child, I was so in tune with what was going on that I could finish Pastor Cannon's message. My mom would have to shush me! In the Pentecostal church, as a child, I had the ability to speak in a heavenly language, as I do today. Fast forward to age twenty with much life being lived in between, I was sitting at home on my living room couch. I had been faithfully attending church, no drinking, smoking, or even wearing pants at the time! I simply from my heart asked God, "What's missing?"

I don't know what was different about this time, but it's as if he said to me, "Ask me to come into your heart." So simple yet so profound. After all my searching, doing, and going through the motions, all it took was sincerity. So I did. I asked Him to come into my heart, and He DID! I didn't have any goosebumps, just a simple peace. I felt a richness and love that's indescribable. So my journey was not out of fear of going to hell. It was a soft, quiet intimate answer to my searching heart. He answered me. The question of why I got saved also opened up my attention to principle number 1.

Prayer for Salvation: God, I confess that I am a sinner and I'm in need of a savior. I believe that you sent your son to die in my place. Your only begotten son. I know that my sins cause a separation between me and you. I want to be close to you. I want to know you. I accept what you have done for me. I ask you, in the name of Jesus to come into my heart. Come into my mind, I welcome you. Live in and through me. Use me for your glory. I ask that you forgive me of my sins. I receive your forgiveness. I am now saved! Now that I'm a member of your family, God, I thank you that I have now passed from death to life. Use my life to bring glory to your name and your kingdom. Give me a mind-set to learn of you, to fellowship with you continually. Thank you, Father. In Jesus's name, I pray, Amen!

Notes

PRINCIPLE NUMBER 1

Right Foundation for Building a Godly Life

A foundation defined by Merriam Webster is something (such as an idea, a principle, or a fact) that provides support for something. A foundation is the base for something. A foundation supports something else. A foundation has to be strong enough to support what will be built on top of it. If your salvation foundation is fear, then what's built on top of it will crumble and be distorted. Your view is skewed. Whatever teaching that brings believers to Christ from a spirit of fear is not the good news of Christ. We must go back and revisit our base. Our belief system, how we see God, and how we respond to God. We must learn His nature and His character. The truth is that we are born in sin. Not because of our own doing, but because of what happened in the Garden of Eden. We were born separated from God and we needed our fellowship restored since it was broken in the garden. That's why we needed to be saved. But God commendeth his love toward us, in that, while we were yet sinners, Christ died for us (Romans 5:8 KJV). John 3:16 says, "For God so loved the world, that he gave his only begotten Son, that whosoever believeth in him should not perish, but have everlasting life." This shows the love of God. No fear is here. As God has provided everything from a position of love, we should accept his provision from a heart of love. Salvation is deliverance from sin and its consequence, which the penalty of sin is separation from God. The offer of salvation usually is presented after a fire and brimstone message or one that is laced with "You're going to hell!" No wonder, many believers have accepted the call in fear! Most believers think that God is an angry task master. That he's waiting to punish them when they do something wrong. Some believe that God will leave and abandon them. The Bible clearly tells us that God will never leave us or forsake us (Deuteronomy 31:6). Others think that they have to be perfect and do everything right! What a life of torment! A relationship with God that is built on fear, will always have you trying to figure out a way of escape because you don't see God as a loving Father. The Bible says in 2 Timothy 1:7, "For God hath not given us a spirit of fear; but of power, and of love, and of a sound mind." Yet, most believers do not live victorious lives or have any manifestations of God's glory. To revisit my foundation, first,

I must see Jesus and what he has done for me. He is the sacrifice for my sin. Our foundation must be built upon love. When we start with love, we have the advantage point. We start from a place of victory. Love is the greatest command we have. What God did for us came from love. I have to see him through the lenses of love. And above all things have fervent charity among yourselves: for charity shall cover the multitude of sins (1 Peter 4:8 KJV). Your ground level and starting point for your salvation should be love. We don't have to worry about escaping hell or anything else, but rather focus our life and efforts on the everlasting life that we have received. There is no fear in love. Perfect love expels fear and God loves us perfectly and completely. No need to fear. Fear brings torment.

A prayer to help you have the right foundation: Father God, in the name of Jesus, I have waited for your salvation. I thank you for loving me enough to repair the breach that was between us. I know that my sin hides your face from me. Thank you for repairing the breach. God, I know that you love me and that you long for me. Father, I know you have already made provisions for me throughout eternity to be in your presence. I accept your Son, who died for me in my place. He is your only begotten and you allowed him to be sacrificed in my stead. Father, I thank you for your loving and kind heart. I receive your love right now in my heart. Thank you, God, that I will ever be with you. In Jesus's name, Amen.

Notes

PRINCIPLE 2

Knowing Jesus Right

How do you see Jesus? Most people see him as an ancient person who lived many years ago. Some see him as a prophet only. Some see him as a man who was born of a virgin, who taught multitudes, had disciples, was crucified and died. Although the latter is true, if this is all that we know, then we've missed him. Who is he (present tense)? He is *alive*! Hallelujah! Yes, he was crucified, but he didn't stay there! He got up with all power in his hands! Some who say they are believers, really don't know him. We sit in church, week after week, shout, dance, fellowship with other parishioners, sing in the choir, serve on various boards, yet we really don't know him. We perform all of the religious activities, but we have no fellowship, relationship, or intimacy with him. How then can we know him if we only wait until Sunday morning for a few hours only to seek him. He's not a part and has no part in our daily lives or our plans. It's very difficult and almost impossible to have a relationship with someone you do not communicate with or spend time getting to know. Jesus tells us in Matthew 11:29–30, "Take my yoke upon you, and learn of me; for I am meek and lowly in heart; and ye shall find rest unto your souls. For my yoke is easy, and my burden is light." We are commanded to get to know his thoughts, his plans, his heart, his mind, his way of doing things. His way of responding because we're automatically born with a sin nature. So we have to be transformed and we must renew our minds daily. Only the Word of God will transform us. It's the only thing that has the power to mend a wounded and destitute and depraved soul. Our hearts have to be cleansed, and he's the only one that can do that. As I spend time with him, alone, just one on one, that changes me. I begin to look like him, live like him. When I began to learn of him and from him, he changes me. It's impossible to be in his presence and stay the same. He searches my heart and cleanses it. His shed blood washes me. He reveals how desperately wicked the heart really is, then he cleanses it. His Word tells us in 1 John 1:9, "If we confess our sins, he is faithful and just to forgive us, and to cleanse us from all unrighteousness." This shows one of his attributes. He's faithful and just. The forgiveness of my sins, restores fellowship with him. It's easier to have a relationship with someone where there's no condemnation. Once he allows me to see my sin and I come into agreement with him about my sin, not only does he forgive, but he also cleanses me. Our heart (mind) needs to be cleansed. It's the cleansing the purifying that allows me to know him more intimately. It removes the scab from my heart and allows him to penetrate my mind and regenerate new cells that are like him. His way of being and his way of doing. Oh, the sweet fellowship we can have with our God who wants to be intimate with us. This is the Jesus that I know. Who is lowly and meek. Yet my defender, my savior, my deliverer, my way maker, my friend, my confidant and the lover of my soul! He is my portion, my peace, my strength, my healer, and my restorer. If we have only a Sunday religious relationship with him only, then we merely have a form of godliness, but no power in our lives. God wants to be a part of our everyday activities. While I'm working, I am talking to him or meditating on His word. As I drive along in my car, I'm talking to him. As I cook and clean, I'm talking to him. When I am happy, I talk to him. If I'm concerned or having any issues, I'm talking to him. I commune with him all day every day. He's always on my mind. Not just on Sunday mornings and not just when I need something. Prayer is a gift that he's given to every believer. It's our way to communicate with him and for him to speak back to us. What great joy we should have, just to know that we have the ability to talk to God! The creator of the universe and everything else. Yet we neglect it. We don't often take advantage of the opportunity to talk to God. We go to other people first, and oftentimes, we don't ask God what he thinks about a matter. We do ourselves great harm by not coming to God first! He has the answer, he knows the plans and he wants to be involved in every area of your life. Not just the things that we think are major. How would you feel if your child only spoke to you when they needed something or if they were in trouble? Not so good, I'd imagine. To fellowship with him is to become more and more like him. It's impossible to know him and remain the same. He was bruised, beaten beyond recognition and chastised for me. Why would I not want to truly know him? How could I ignore him, neglect him, or trample under my feet his blood that he so willingly shed for me. For the remission (pardon) of my sin. For scarcely for a righteous man will one die: yet peradventure for a good man some would even dare to die. But God commendeth his love towards us, in that, while we were yet sinners, Christ died for us (Romans 5:7–8 KJV). Who would willingly die for an enemy? That is what he did! This is the loving Jesus that we should strive to know. He's humble and thoughtful. So full of love. So then, who is this Jesus that we claim to know. Jesus is God! In the Holy Trinity, he is identified as the Son of God. Most people think that Jesus came on the scene in the New Testament, as I did up until I was around twenty years old! My goodness! Not only was he in the Old Testament, but since he is God, he's been there since before time began! And God said, "Let us make man in our image, after our likeness: and let him have dominion over the fish of the sea, and over the fowl of the air, over the cattle, and over all the earth, and over every creeping thing that creepeth upon the earth" (Genesis 1:26 KJV). And also, "In the beginning was the Word, and the Word was with God, and the Word was God. The same was in the beginning with God" (John 1:1–2 KJV). You've guessed right, he's talking about Jesus and to Jesus. This same Jesus is in the Old Testament, sometimes referred to as the Angel of the Lord. There is nothing new about him. Behold, he came in the volume of the book Psalm 40:7, In the old covenant, he was prophesied about, wrapped up in the feasts, in the temple, he was concealed. Hidden. In the new covenant, he is revealed. And the word was made flesh, and dwelt among us (and we beheld his glory, the glory as of the only begotten of the Father) full of grace and truth (John 1:14 KJV). He also said in John 12:47, "And if any man hears my words, and believe not, I judge him not: for I came not to judge the world, but to save the world." This is the Jesus that I know. Everything was made by him. As long as God is and will be, so is he. Infinity! He is Ancient of Days. He is not just some prophet who came through the Virgin Mary, He has always existed, just in another form. In Spirit, because he is a Spirit who put on an earthly body. Before the earth was created, he was there. He is eternal, everlasting, and he grants the same thing to us, once we accept who he is. As he is, so are we! We receive the gift of not only salvation, but everlasting life. We don't have to wait until we leave earth to start operating from an eternal position, we already have it! He gave it to us when we believed on him. I am fully victorious now, I don't have to wait to become, I already am. We win! Not when we get to heaven only, but right now. Because of Jesus, we have his same power at work within us. Not only does he save us, but he also brings gifts with him! He is Lord, all knowing and all powerful. He is our reward. He is the author and finisher of our faith. He is our righteousness, our hope. According as his divine power he hath given unto us all things that pertain unto life and godliness, through the knowledge of him that hath called us to glory and virtue (2 Peter 1:3 KJV). I have everything that I need to live a victorious life. I only need to develop and learn of the gifts that he has given me. Jesus is patient and kind. He washes us from the contaminants of life. He heals ours scars, opens our eyes, and gives us strength in our feeble parts, through a process of purging then restoring. He is love in the purest form. He is compassionate, merciful, and passionate for his people. He is always about his father's business and so must we. If the House of God means something to him, it must be important to us. If he studied the scripture and attending to the temple was his custom, so must it be ours also. We have to take the time to learn what's important to him and the order of importance. That's why it's so vital to our lives to spend time getting to know him. He is our high priest and our intercessor. He leads us, makes us lie down when we need to, protects us, fills us, anoints us all while preparing a table before us! He is ever present when trouble comes, he hides us under wings in his secret place, replenishes our souls, and protects us from dangers seen and unseen. As he led the children of Israel through the wilderness, so does he continue leading us through our wilderness like situations. He's always there. He is the only constant in our lives. This is knowing Jesus correctly. The more you know Him, the more you will love and appreciate him.

A prayer to know him correctly: Father God, in the name of Jesus, your Word says in Hebrews 11:6 that without faith, it is impossible to please him: for he that cometh to God must believe that he is, and that he is a rewarder of them that diligently seek him. Father, as I began to seek you diligently, your Word says that you will reward me. Father, reward me with a better understanding of you. Help me to see you more clearly and correctly. Remove any false unrighteous and distorted views that I may have knowingly or unknowingly of you. Remove religion from me and show me you. In the name of Jesus, I do pray. Amen.

Notes

PRINCIPLE 3

~

Right Perception

How do you see yourself? When asked this question, most people will respond with all sorts of answers even though they have never really thought about it. If you ask a hundred people, I'm certain you will have a hundred different answers. Some see themselves as their title. For example, mother, father, teacher, actor, etc. Most people identify themselves by what they do. We have to learn to have the correct perception about ourselves. Most of us see ourselves and define ourselves from what we have been through. We see the scars and hurts. We define ourselves through the eyes of pain, emptiness, rejection, anger, fear, guilt, and condemnation. Our self-esteem and self-worth are low most often as a result of the aforementioned. Often times, we do not see ourselves as God sees us do to sin, unbelief, and lack of a relationship with him. If Jesus thought enough of us, better yet, loved us so much, that he was willing to die and be raised up again for us, should not we know that we have value? Think about that. Jesus thought I was to die for! Jesus left glory, to bring us back into right standing with himself, was beaten, despised and crucified for us, and yet we still see ourselves as unworthy. There was none able to redeem us, but he provided the answer. He is the answer. Who being in the form of God, thought it not robbery to be equal with God: But made himself of no reputation, and took upon him the form of a servant, and was made in the likeness of men (Philippians 2:6–7 KJV). We are so precious in his sight, that he came and was tempted in all ways as we are, yet without sin. For we have not a high priest which cannot be touched with the feeling of our infirmities; but was in all points tempted like as we are, yet without sin (Hebrews 4:15 KJV). God knows exactly what you're going through. In order to perceive right, we must continually dedicate ourselves to prayer. Prayer allows us to see God in another way. God speaking to the God in us is a magnificent thing. To have the ability to commune with God all day long, just as Adam did before the fall is the greatest gift man has. Deep intimate prayer truly transcends time, space, dimensions, the galaxies, and everything else. Prayer takes me to the very throne of God. And no one, no demon, power, principality, ruler of darkness, spiritual wickedness, or Satan himself can stop me from communicating with God. Having the right perception is developed through prayer, hearing the very heart of God, getting insight that only comes from him. When the Holy Spirit speaks for you and through you, then the word enters into the human heart and mind. Being disciplined in prayer and consistency opens up the eternal life that we've already received. Right perception says that I will not die but live, therefore I don't have to fear dying. God understands your disappointments. Just because you have struggles and hurts that doesn't disqualify you from being valuable, in fact that's what qualifies you. You are precious in his sight. He loves you with an everlasting love. He's there in the midst, and he's the only person who will deliver on the promise that he'll never leave nor forsake you. Please don't define yourself by what you have been through. What you did not receive or any unfair disadvantage. God came for the sick, those who are captive by life and sin. He came just for you! Is there any defeat in Jesus? No! Is there any lack in Jesus? No! See yourself as he is, victorious. He is an overcomer and so are we. Is he full of peace? Yes, and so are you. Is he obedient and full of love and patience? Yes, so are you. Begin to see yourself as he is. Remember, he's given us all things. Begin to see yourself as an agent of change. Change in your family, your community, your place of employment, your business, your church, and your world. Begin to see yourself as one who is slow to anger and suffers long. See yourself as being full of his spirit who has the ability to discern matters, full of wisdom, knowledge, and revelation. See yourself as someone who never walks alone. Develop a picture in your mind of yourself being whole, complete, and lacking no good thing. See yourself as the righteousness of God because you are! See yourself being free from all shackles and chains that have held you back. No longer do you need approval and affirmations from others. God has already affirmed you. You are now free to be who he has called you to be. You're also free to do what he's given you do to. When God saved you, he gave you an assignment. Fulfill your assignment. Seek him to know what that assignment is. Vision yourself walking in your purpose and enjoying the fruit that comes along with that! Peace and joy. See yourself as unstoppable, backed by heaven's army with the universe backing you because Almighty God is with you, in you, and for you! You are unshakeable and unmovable because God is with you. You have more value and power than you know! See yourself living the life that Jesus was resurrected for you to have, the newness of life. You are changing, growing, and being made to be presented perfect without any spots, wrinkles, or blemishes. In Number 13:33, we see the children of Israel seeing themselves as grasshoppers in the sight of their enemy. Their perception of themselves was so low, that they believed their enemy saw them the same way! The Word of God tells us that we are fearfully and wonderfully made. We have to renew our minds with the Word of God. That is what changes our perception. What does the word say about me? David was a smaller man in stature when it came to Goliath, but he was stronger in his faith! Allow God's word to become the supreme ruler in your life. That's why it's important to ruminate on the Word of God.

It's the most important tool we have, the answer for all of life's issues, yet we spend the least amount of time in it. Filling my mind with the Word of God changes my perception because as he is higher than we are, so are his ways, his thoughts, and the way he operates. We have to grow in the way we perceive things. Even our trials. If we believe God is against us and not for us, when we're faced with tragedies or not so good news, we can easily slip into despair or depression. Because we don't have the right view of God. If you are bold and you really want to grow in your relationship with God, ask him to allow you to see yourself as he sees you! I guarantee that will awaken something in your spirit. It takes courage to ask this question because you may not like what he shows you. It may be a painful revelation, but it is the groundwork for having a right perception.

Prayer for right perception: Father God, in the name of Jesus, I thank you for allowing me to see myself as you see me. I thank you for looking beyond my faults and meeting me at the very place of my need. Father, I thank you for allowing me to see myself through your eyes and conforming me into your glorious image. In Jesus's name I pray, Amen.

Notes

PRINCIPLE 4

Believing Right

In this walk through our spiritual journey, we can have wrong beliefs. There are wrong teachings that have gone forth into the world, along with false prophets and teachers. Lying spirits and deceptive tongues are also in operation. That is why it is necessary for us to have the Holy Spirit. He leads us and guides us into all truth. He will not allow us to be deceived. The Holy Spirit is our teacher, our guide, and He illuminate God's Word for us. He gives us the understanding. This is why it is important to have an intimate relationship with God. He does not allow us to be ignorant of the devices and schemes from the enemy. It's because of him that we are in tune spiritually. Without his leading, we are open to being led and drawn away, according to Ephesians 4:14 KJV, "That we henceforth be no more children, tossed to and fro, and carried about with every wind of doctrine, by the sleight of men, and cunning craftiness, whereby they lie in wait to deceive." The Holy Spirit helps us to believe right. We can be deceived and not even know it. The Word tells us in 1 John 4:1, "Beloved, believe not every spirit, but try the spirits whether they are of God: because many false prophets are gone out into the world." Matthew 24:24 tells us, "For there shall arise false Christs, and false prophets, and shall shew great signs and wonders; insomuch that, if it were possible, they shall deceive even the very elect." The false prophets and erroneous teachers have one thing in mind, and that is to deceive. Without the help of the Holy Spirit, we cannot believe right. Right believing is critical because your life will flow and align itself with what you believe. Wrong believing will have you thinking that God is mad at you, that he's out to get you or that you have to perform a certain way to be saved. Wrong believing will have you thinking that you have to go to a certain church, on a certain day, wear this or that. Wrong believing says that I have to earn God's love and that God is unjust. Wrong believing says that I'm supposed to be sick, poor, and suffering. That I'm a victim, no one loves me, and that I'm unworthy of love, good breaks, favor, and good things in my life. That this is God's will for my life, when his Word actually declares different. For as a man thinketh in his heart/mind, so is he: "Eat and drink, saith he to thee; but his heart is not with thee" (Psalm 23:7 KJV.) It is vitally important that we watch we allow ourselves to think. We must identify our hurts and the things that have injured us and seek God's healing from those things. If left untreated, those things will poison our beliefs. Our very lives depend on it. For instance, if you believe that it's okay to be treated less than, you will always settle for less because you don't believe you deserve better. If you believe that you will always be poor, then guess what? You will always be poor. Right believing starts with rightly understanding the Word of God. You must spend time in prayer, in Bible studies, giving ourselves to time with God. Meditating, blocking out all of life's issues. Shutting down our minds with periods of rest, stillness, and quietness. Through his word, we learn of him. He said in Matthew 11:29, "Take my yoke upon you, and learn of me; for I am meek and lowly in heart: and ye shall find rest for your souls." Studying the holy scriptures is how we transform our believing. It gives our minds rest. We know his thoughts are not ours, neither are his ways our ways. We have to be transformed. It takes faith to believe right. We learn to trust that what he has spoken, he will to bring to pass. According to Numbers 23:19, "God is not a man, that he should lie; neither the son of man, that he should repent: hath he said, and shall he not do it? Or hath he spoken, and shall he not make it good?" It takes faith to believe. We believe and have not seen him. In John 20:29 KJV, Jesus saith unto him, "Thomas, because thou hast seen me, thou hast believed: blessed are they that have not seen, yet have believed." We do not hope for what we see. We hope for what we cannot see. That takes faith. We see through the eyes of faith. We have an assurance on

31

the inside of us, the Holy Spirit that helps us in our belief. Hope against hope. Right believing based on God's Word. When you come to a fork in the road and you're not sure which way to go, check God's Word and or simply ask the Holy Spirit living on the inside of you, you can ask him for yourself. We are to be careful of whom we seek counsel from as believers, because we do not want to end up in a ditch! Wrong believing and not studying will have you fighting in places where you have no authority. Listening to people only and not studying will have you thinking that you're supposed to fight with demons. We are not told anywhere in scripture to fight demons. We are told to cast them out. Study to shew thyself approved unto God, a workman that needeth not to be ashamed, rightly dividing the word of truth (2 Timothy 2:15 KJV). Right believing tells me that no matter what I'm facing, that we know all things work together for good to them that love God, to them who are the called according to his purpose (Romans 8:28 KJV). When I believe right, I start from a place of victory. I don't have to wait until the battle is over to rejoice, I rejoice always, because I've spent time in God's word. In his presence and I've invested intimate time learning of him as he has commanded. Because I renew my mind daily, I believe right. Right believing tells me, that I never walk alone. Even if I'm in the valley, God is there. If I'm in a fiery furnace, God is there. If I'm happy he's there, if I'm sad, he's there. Through it all, I know he's there. He gives me confidence and peace. When he tells me to be still and hold my peace, I believe him. My belief is not predicated on what I see or how I feel. You have to know that you know at all times and through all seasons. Right believing tells me to trust him even when I don't understand what's going on. In times when he's silent, I know that he's still working. During the dark and difficult times of our lives, we have to truly seek not to put our weight on our own understanding because our understanding is limited.

A prayer for right belief: Father God, in the name of Jesus, help me to trust you and believe in you when times are tough. Father, it's in those tough moments where our belief is tested. Help me to not fail, turn away, or run during my time of testing. Thank you for initiating the relationship and helping me to believe in you rightly. In the name of Jesus, Amen.

Notes

PRINCIPLE 5

Having the Right Faith

As mentioned in chapter 4, having the right faith is vital to a believer. Faith is complete trust or confidence in someone or something. It also is a strong belief in God or in the doctrines (teachings) of a religion, based on spiritual apprehension (understanding) rather than proof. Our belief comes from God first and foremost. Our confidence and complete trust is in him. Jesus said in Mark 11:22, "And Jesus answering said, Have faith in God." To receive anything that God has for us, we must first receive it by faith. Notice that he did not say for us to have faith in our job, our riches, or anything else. Partly because when things happen or are taken from us, He remains. If we have faith in him, we know that we will recover. Things in life are sometimes shaken. Relationships, businesses fail, markets crash, loved one's transition, but the only constant is him. Right faith says, that I believe him. My assurance is in him and his finished work on the cross. Faith tells me that I've been bought with a price and since he paid for me with his shed blood, surely he will take care of me. He will meet my needs and provide for me. I am totally and completely dependent upon him. Sometimes as humans, we misplace our faith. We put our faith in people who let us down, institutions that fail us, and in the world's system of doing things which almost always lead to devastation. Sometimes, being vulnerable, we can even put our complete trust in to spiritual leaders and are sometimes taken advantage of. Wrong faith can have you believing for someone else's spouse! We covet other people's lifestyle, not really knowing what's going on beyond closed doors. It's dangerous to have misplaced faith. We are commanded to believe, trust, and have confidence in God. Not our looks, our wardrobe, our homes, or even our cars. Things on earth corrode, are stolen, fade, burn, and get old. We should not put our faith in things. We must lean and depend on God. God is not fickle neither does he change with the weather. Jesus Christ is the same yesterday, and today, and forever, according to Hebrews 13:8 KJV. He does not change, disappear, or waver. We can trust that he knows all of our deepest secrets, fears, and insecurities, yet he will not share them with any one. He sees us in our condition and he loves us. There is no self-preservation with him! With faith, we can declare how things will be. God allows us the ability to make a decree, he will even back it up! When our faith is activated, turned on, we operate in another realm. We are strong and encouraged when will live by faith. Seeing something in the natural does not take faith. We don't physically see Jesus, but by faith, we believe that he is and that he exists. The right faith produces a peace that passes all understanding. The right faith produces a rest in the soul, where you're not anxious. Human and natural understanding can't understand faith. Faith is contrary to human reasoning. Faith is greater than understanding, it's on a different level. Faith produces rewards! The right faith moves God, the right faith pleases God. To know that I have the ability to please God! It moves him to see me operating in faith. In him seeing that I have complete and total confidence in him stirs him to act. Just because I believe he will and that he can! Even if he chooses not to. But without faith, it is impossible to please God: for he that cometh to God must believe that he is, and that he is a rewarder of them that diligently seek him (Hebrews 11:6 KJV). Wow, when God sees faith it pleases Him. Oh, to have the Creator pleased with me! God gives each of us a measure of faith. We can grow it and cause it to become greater, or it can stay little! Having right faith is a keeper. Faith demolishes worry and fear. Faith says that before I entered the world, God had all of the answers for everything I would encounter. Just as the garden was prepared for Adam and Eve, so are my provisions. Where is your faith? Where have you placed it? I want to encourage you to think back and find out where you put it down and pick it up! Faith is a powerful tool that the believer has. It's a currency. It gives us access to places we wouldn't in our own ability be able to reach, so much so that the word tells us to walk by it. Faith causes a response. A chain of events take place when we operate in faith. Faith brings us into agreement with God. We live by it. The just shall live by faith (Romans 1:17 KJV). It takes faith to enter the family of God and it takes faith to live in the family of God. There are some who can't believe supernaturally because they have to see it first, they have to know all of the plans in advance, they can't see or believe supernaturally. They are limited to this dimension only. Faith says, "God, I believe you no matter what." Like the three Hebrew boys, faith says, "If it be so, our God whom we serve is able to deliver us from the fiery furnace, and he will deliver us out of thine hand, O king" (Daniel 3:17 KJV). Faith is exercised in challenging situations. In my journey as a believer, I realize looking back twenty years ago when I received Jesus into my heart, I was on FIRE! It's as if I could call down fire from heaven and God would answer me immediately! When first starting out, God would answer me very fast when I prayed, well, that was then, when I was new to faith. Twenty years later, God does not always answer as fast. Now, I've learned to trust him, while I wait. He's answered, it just sometimes takes longer for the promise to manifest. In the beginning, my faith was small. I think it's good for me that he doesn't answer so quickly. I couldn't stay on milk. I had to get to where I can eat and digest meat. We have to grow in our faith. There are different levels of faith. I remember going through a legal matter a few years ago, a terrible thing had happened. I remember speaking with the district attorney who was over the case. I told her, this is what's going to happen… God is not going to allow this…to happen. A few days later, she called me and the first thing out of her mouth was "Mrs. Johnson, you have great faith!" It's amazing when a person who may not believe like you do, tells you that you have great faith. Great faith occurs where the opposition is great. The greater the opposition, the deeper the depth of our faith. It takes a special someone to believe in the impossible. That's why there are many unbelievers in our world. They are tied to their five senses. It has to make sense naturally. Some think we live in la-la-land because our belief is different. We're not limited by what we see, in fact we look beyond what we see. We understand that there is more at work that what we see. Crazy faith! When we live out our faith, others do see it. It's not in vain when we go through our times of testing. Your faith will be tested. What you profess and make known, will be tested. But testing is good. Testing strengthens the believer. Remember, Jesus was tested also. 1 Peter 4:12 says, "Beloved, think it not strange concerning the fiery trial which is to try you, as though some strange thing happened to you." Knowing this, that the trying of your faith worketh patience (James 1:3). We need the patience so we can learn to wait on God. According to 1 Corinthians 1:27, "But God hath chosen the foolish things of the world to confound the wise, and God hath chosen the weak things of the world to confound the things which are mighty." Whatever your measure of faith is, use it for your advancement. God wants us to have faith in him. He wants to move in our lives in a mighty way, but a lack of faith stays his hand. Having the right faith adds on to the quality of your life. Having and operating in faith distinguishes you from others. People will be able to tell by your lifestyle that you are a person of faith. Faith speak for itself. It has its own language.

A prayer for right faith: Father God, in the name of Jesus, thank you for giving me faith. You are the author and the finisher of my faith. You began and you will finish what you have started. Thank you for allowing me an opportunity to please you. You mean so much to me. Thank you, in Jesus's name, Amen.

Notes

PRINCIPLE 6

~

Right Thinking

I'll start by asking a question. What's on your mind right now? Job said, "For the thing which I greatly feared is come upon me, and that which I was afraid of is come unto me" (Job 3:25 KJV). It appears that Job may have thought about this before it happened. It's very important what we allow ourselves to think about. We must guard our thinking diligently. We are urged to think on whatever things are true, whatsoever things are honest, whatsoever things are just, whatsoever things are lovely, whatsoever things are of good report; if there be any virtue, and if there be any praise, think on these things (Philippians 4:8 KJV). These are the things we should think on and ponder. Whatever you allow to occupy your mind is what you will have. If you're thinking wrong and negative, that is what's going to manifest in your life. As we take out the trash in our natural house, so must we empty the trash in our thinking. We are not to fill our thoughts with negativity or even evil. Sometimes, you have to just change the channel. Wrong thinking leads to depression, anger, confusion, and all kinds of ungodliness. Everything manifested and our actions, started with a thought. If you don't want to hold it in your hand, don't hold it in your mind! Is what you're thinking about what you want, if not, change your thinking. Oftentimes, we go through life, not paying attention to what we allow our minds to think about. We are to bring every thought captive. Our thoughts are not supposed to run away with us. As a matter of fact, the Word tells us to cast down imaginations, and every high thing that exalts itself against the knowledge of God, and bringing every thought captive to the obedience of Christ (2 Corinthians 10:5). We are to actively control what we entertain in our mind. Thoughts are powerful. We have to be on thought patrol. Trolling our thinking. Meaning, pay attention constantly to what we are thinking about. Sadness and depression comes from thinking too long on the wrong thing, things you have no control over. We often don't recognize that our thinking is off until we find ourselves, irritable, overwhelmed, and stressed, which forces us to back track and reassess our thinking. We must become aware of our thinking. Chances are, wherever you are right now in your life, it is a result of your thinking. Well, the good news is that all you have to do is change your thinking! Get a better image in your mind, and think on that. The Bible says be not conformed to this world, but be ye transformed by the renewing of your mind, that ye may prove what is that good, and acceptable and perfect will of God. When we renew our minds with the word of God, it changes our thinking. It transforms us and we're able to prove the good, acceptable, and perfect will of God (Romans 12:2 KJV). For to be carnally minded (of or relating to physical, especially sexual needs and activities) is death: but to be spiritually minded is life and peace. Because the carnal mind is enmity against God: for it is not subject to the law of God, neither indeed can be (Romans 8:6–7 KJV). As much as possible, strive to be spiritually minded, there's life and peace. Sometimes, we just need a spiritual viewpoint to elevate our thinking. Repenting is simply changing your mind and getting back to the top. Turning and deciding to go in the opposite direction. If you are not getting the results you want out of life, check your thinking. Evaluate your decision making process and how you arrive at certain conclusions. The Lord tells us in Isaiah 1:18, "Come now, and let us reason together, saith the Lord: though your sins be as scarlet, they shall be as white as snow; though they be red like crimson, they shall be as wool." God wants to talk with us and change our thinking. He will lead the way, he is our guide, if we allow him. Our way of thinking leads to separation from God. Wrong thinking leads to wrong decision making. Your thoughts become your reality. As a soldier guards a fort, so likewise, guard your thoughts. Check to see if your thoughts line up with the Word of God, His way of thinking and being. We must fill our minds with good things in order for our life to produce the right fruit.

Prayer for right thinking: Father God, in the name of Jesus, I submit my thoughts to you. I ask you to lead me in my thinking. I yield myself to learning of you, your word and your righteousness. Thank you, Lord, for helping me to monitor my thinking and causing me to elevate where I need to. In the name of Jesus, Amen.

Notes

PRINCIPLE 7

Having the Right Vision

Most of us have sight, we can see with our natural eyes, but we have no vision for our life. Jesus said in John 10:10b, "I am come that they might have life, and that they may have it more abundantly." Get that vision of what Jesus said. He came that they might have life and have it more abundantly. Allow the vision to settle in your mind, a life of abundance. Part of having the abundantly life, you must be a giver. For God so loved the world that he gave. God loves cheerful givers. People who share what they have. Luke 6:38 says, "Give, and it shall be given unto you; good measure, pressed down, and shaken together, and running over, shall men give into your bosom. For with the same measure that you mete withal it shall be measured to you again." This principle says that whatever you give, it will be given unto more. It starts with seeing yourself as a giver. Whether you need money, peace, love, joy, support, or whatever, give it, and it will be given unto you in abundance. To receive anything, you have to give something. You will get what you give. That is a principle. You reap what you have sown. So sow wisely and in abundance. It will be measured back in the spirit in which you gave. What do you see spiritually that is waiting to manifest in your life? Most of us go through life with no vision. Vision is something that you imagine, an image. What image are you holding in your mind? If you don't have one, grab a hold of one and keep it in the forefront of your mind until it comes to pass. Without a vision, we perish. We go around in circles lost like a ship with no sail. Driven and tossed by the winds, ending up wherever the wind blows. Your life has purpose and meaning. Ask God what is your purpose and the vision that he has for your life. Understanding your purpose gives you vision. An area where you can target your focus and energy. Jesus gave sight to the blind and he's still doing it today. If you have no vision or direction for your life, if you feel as if your life has no meaning, simply ask God to open your eyes so that you can see, his will, purpose, and plan for your life. Vision brings life. With the vision, God will bring others to help you bring it to pass. God's vision is so big that you will need help! God wants to open your spiritual eyes to the plan that he has for you. In Jeremiah 29:11, it says, "For I know the thoughts that I think towards you, saith the Lord, thoughts of peace, and not of evil, to give you an expected end." God has the vision, we need only to come into agreement with him for the revelation.

God's thoughts do come to pass! Amen. Having the right vision is a guide for your life. It will lead you to where you need to be. The steps of a good man are ordered by the Lord, the Bible says in Psalm 37:23. Every believer should have a vision from God. It's discovered through fellowship and relationship with him. All of the plans belong to God. He has them, he knows, and he wants to pour into your life. As he pours into you, you will become so full that you will automatically pour into others. My cup runs over. Vision yourself as a cheerful and faithful giver. Start where you are. Part of discovering the vision for your life, look at your passions, the thing that really brings joy to your spirit, the thing that when you do it, you enter into another realm, the earth can't contain you. That's a strong indicator.

Prayer for the right vision for your life: Father God in the name of Jesus, I ask that you restore my sight. The areas of my life where I've been blind. Father, I ask you to supernaturally remove the scale from my eyes. Lord Jesus, anoint my eyes that I may see as you and the plans that you have for my life. In Jesus's name, Amen.

Notes

ABOUT THE AUTHOR

A mother of two children, a son and a daughter. Raised in Dallas, Texas. A devoted believer in Jesus Christ who has a passion for God's word and seeing people reach their full potential. Sakeanah Johnson is a woman of strong faith. She believes in encouraging the downtrodden and bringing hope to every situation. She's a light in a land of darkness. Her faith has opened many doors for her and continues to drive her forward. She is a preacher and strong teacher of God's Holy Word. She is set apart for God's use, and she takes her calling very seriously. A woman full of love and compassion. She's selfless and giving. She believes in giving back to the less fortunate and serving her community.